TRANSPORT

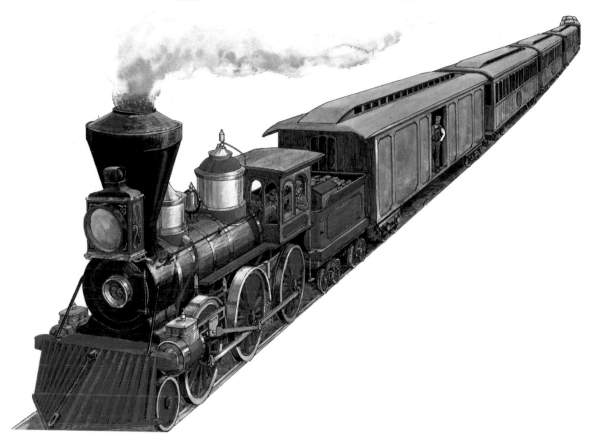

ON LAND, ROAD & RAIL

Series Editor:
David Salariya was born in Dundee, Scotland, where he studied illustration and printmaking, concentrating on book design in his postgraduate year. He later completed a further post-graduate course in art education at Sussex University in England. He has illustrated a wide range of books on botanical, historical, and mythical subjects. He has designed and created many new series of children's books for publishers in the U.K. and overseas. In 1989, he established his own publishing company, The Salariya Book Company, Ltd. He lives in Brighton, England, with his wife, illustrator Shirley Willis.

Author:
Eryl Davies is a curator in the Science Museum, London. He has written books and articles on a wide variety of subjects, ranging from undersea technology to communications. He has worked as a script consultant for a television series called *The Secret Lives of Machines*. His interests include scuba diving and music.

Series Editor	David Salariya
Senior Editor	Ruth Taylor
Assistant Editor	Rachel Bennington

Artists	Mark Bergin
	Nick Hewetson
	John James
	Wendy Meadway
	Hans Wiborg-Jenssen
	Gerald Wood

First published in 1992
by Franklin Watts

Artists
Mark Bergin, p 8-9, p 22-23, p 30-31, p 32-33, p 36-37, p 38-39, p 40-41, p 42-43; **Nick Hewetson**, p 4-5; **John James**, p 10-11, p 12-13, p 18-19; **Wendy Meadway**, p 20-21, p 34-35; **Hans Wiborg-Jenssen**, p 28-29 ; **Gerald Wood**, p 6-7, p 14-15, p 16-17, p 24-25, p 26-27.

©The Salariya Book Co Ltd MCMXCII

Library of Congress Cataloging-in-Publication Data

Davies, Eryl.
    Transport / by Eryl Davies.
        p. cm. - (Timelines)
    Includes index.
    Summary. Surveys the development of land transportation in relation to the needs, skills, and technologies of people living at different periods of history.
    ISBN 0-531 -15244-8.
    1. Transportation - Juvenile literature.
    2. Transportation - History.
    1. Series: Timelines (Franklin Watts, Inc.)
TA1149. D38 1992
629. 04'9 -- dc20   91 -10942
                                            CIP   AC

Printed in Belgium

TIMELINES
TRANSPORT

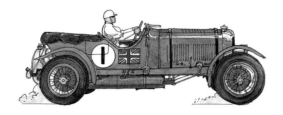

ON LAND, ROAD & RAIL

Written by
ERYL DAVIES

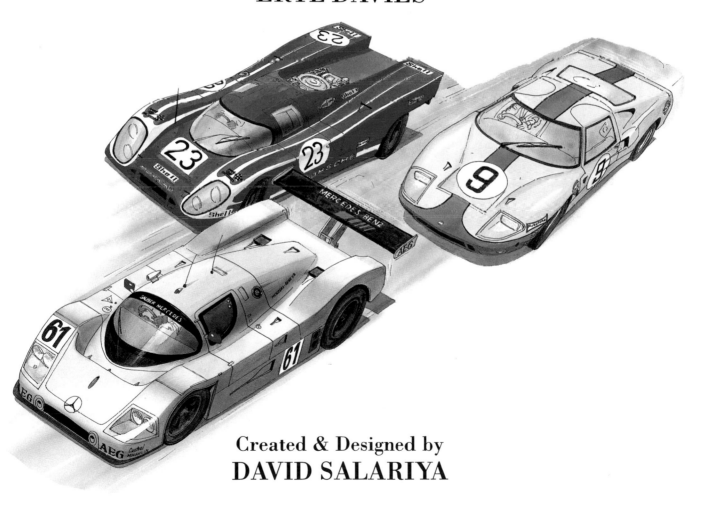

Created & Designed by
DAVID SALARIYA

FRANKLIN WATTS
New York • London • Toronto • Sydney

CONTENTS

THE FIRST WHEELS

VEHICLES EXISTED before wheels were invented. Crude sleds (*left*), often made from the branches of a tree, were used for moving objects that were too heavy to be carried. Large stone blocks for building were more easily moved by rolling them end over end. The introduction of the potter's wheel eventually led to the development of wheels for transport. Archaeologists are certain that they were first used in Sumeria (now Iraq) in about 3500 B.C. The Sumerians were so advanced, and had so many new ideas and inventions that the region is known as the Cradle of Civilization. Primitive art from Sumeria shows sleds adapted to run on wheels, and various kinds of wagons, carts, and chariots. These vehicles were used for taking soldiers into battle, as well as everyday transport.

△ A MODEL of a covered wagon from 3000 B.C., found in a tomb in Tepe Gawra, Assyria (north Iraq).

▽ TWO SUMERIAN WHEELS: a three-part wooden disk with studs (*left*) and one with a copper rim.

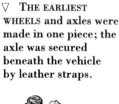

▽ THE EARLIEST WHEELS and axles were made in one piece; the axle was secured beneath the vehicle by leather straps.

◁ VEHICLES are shown in ancient art, such as on this Sumerian vase, pre-2500 B.C.

△ A MODEL of a four-wheeled wagon from a Cretan tomb, around 2000 B.C.

△ TWO-WHEELED CART in a limestone carving from Ur, Mesopotamia, 2500 B.C.

▷ WHEELWRIGHT making a wooden wheel; a felloe is being fitted into the rim.

△ SUMERIAN CHARIOTS from the *Royal Standard of Ur* mosaic. These lumbering four-wheelers were drawn by onagers (wild asses). They were used as troop carriers rather than fighting platforms.

Neither horses nor chariots had been seen in Egypt until about 1600 B.C., when the country was invaded by the Hyksos, a neighboring Middle-Eastern tribe. Subsequently the Egyptians started to copy their invaders' vehicles. After 1300 B.C. the Hittites defeated the Egyptians with chariot attacks. The Egyptians then found ways of making chariots lighter and stronger. These ancient war machines were as important as tanks in modern armies.

△ COMPLETE CHARIOTS were found in Egypt where they had been interred in tombs with their owner. Decorations from the Chariot of Thothmes IV, 1420 B.C.

△ DRAWING FROM A TOMB in Thebes, 1475 B.C. Egyptian wheels were strong, light, and had four or six spokes. Their one-piece wooden rims were formed by heating the wood.

◁ PHARAOH RAMESES II in his chariot, clashing with the Hittites at Kadesh, 1286 B.C. Egyptian chariots were very light, fast, and nimble.

△ CARRYING A DRIVER and an archer, chariots were used to swoop down on the enemy's front line, weakening them before the main attack by the infantry.

By 1000 B.C. chariots had appeared in ancient Greece. A model four-wheeled cart which dates back to 2000 B.C. was discovered in a Cretan tomb. Chariots traveled well on flat battlefields but with difficulty elsewhere, as there were no roads or bridges. Vehicles usually had to be unloaded or dismantled before crossing rough ground or rivers.

▽ A GREEK WARRIOR preparing to leave for battle in his chariot. In Greece, chariots were also important in times of peace because they were used for sport as well as war. Chariot racing became great entertainment at the games at Olympus and at Delphi.

▷ A GREEK LEKYTHOS (vase) from 540 B.C. showing a cart in a wedding procession. The wheel does not have spokes radiating from a hub, as on the chariot (top left).

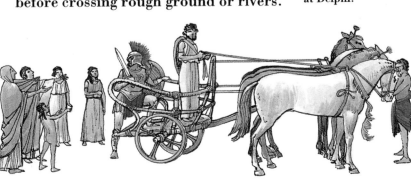

ROMAN ROADS

△ ROMAN CHARIOTEERS were skilled horsemen capable of feats like standing on a horse's back at high speed.

△ THE ROMANS were great surveyors and made maps of roads; (*above*) a milestone from Hadrian's time.

UPKEEP of the Roman road network only lasted while there was a need for it. In A.D.476 the Empire crumbled. Roads were neglected and finally abandoned.

△ AN IRON SHOE for protecting animals' hooves from rough stone road surfaces.

THE ROMANS were among the first people to build and operate a road transport system. As well as being great empire-builders, they were fine engineers. They made particular progress in road- and bridge-building and in the overall organization and usage of their road network. As the Roman influence spread over the Alps beyond Italy and into Spain and Britain, and to the East, it was essential to establish routes for trade, for moving troops and to keep control of distant territories. The first, and best-known, Roman road was the Via Appia, built in 312 B.C. It was 36 feet wide and ran south from Rome to Capua, a distance of 162 miles. Produce from the countryside poured into Rome, in exchange for manufactured items and exotic goods from abroad. Other roads followed in quick succession, and by Hadrian's time (A.D. 117-138) good roads reached from northern Europe to the middle East. Traffic moved at about 5 mph and there were rest houses roughly every 37 miles.

A huge variety of vehicles were used by the Romans. Light goods were sent by packhorse or by mule, while heavier items were carried in lumbering wagons drawn by oxen or mules. Poor people could travel between towns in large four-wheeled coaches, while the wealthy enjoyed the privacy of a two-wheeled carpentum. For short journeys, a lightweight gig called a cisium, driven by a slave, could carry one or two passengers. The Romans were the first people to suffer traffic congestion. So many people took to the roads that laws had to be passed to give priority to military and official traffic. In many cities, vehicles were banned during the day. One way around this was to be carried by slaves in a covered box called a *litter*.

△ SURVEYORS marking out the route. They used an instrument called a *groma*.

△ BUILDING A ROMAN ROAD: a trench is dug along the route and filled in with a foundation of stone blocks laid on sand. Layers of chalk, sand, and broken bricks or chippings support the top surface of the road, which is made of flat stones or gravel. The surface has a camber, with drainage ditches on either side, so that the road does not become awash after heavy rains.

A pole-chariot.

ANCIENT CHINA

IT IS NOW KNOWN that the Chinese made great progress in road-building before the Romans. Chinese silk traders, who traveled in the Middle East, took home news of the wheel around 1500 B.C. In the Chou and Qin Dynasties (1120-221 and 221-207 B.C.) a road and canal network was built in China. These roads were in some ways better than Roman ones, ranging from simple tracks to highways, with special lanes set aside for important traffic. Traffic laws dictated speed limits, priorities at junctions, and standards and weights for vehicle construction.

▽ A CHINESE BRONZE CHARIOT found in 1980.

▽ MANY SLENDER SPOKES were used; Chinese wheels were also dished, making them more resistant to sideways forces.

The Chinese abandoned their roads in about A.D. 300. Some old routes have survived, and since 1974, startling details of carts and chariots have been found in the Qin ruler's tomb.

▷ THE TOMB of Qin Shih Hwang-ti, c.258 to 210 B.C., at Mount Li in northern China contained thousands of life-sized painted terracotta statues of warriors and horses, along with their chariots. The tomb was discovered during the 1970s.

◁ IN THE SOIL around the tomb, impressions of wooden chariots were found; this one is reconstructed from that evidence.

VIKINGS

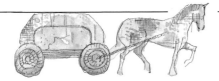

△ A TAPESTRY from Oseberg shows ropes linking cart axles to a horse's harness.

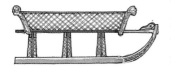

△ SLEDS traveled well over grass or mud, but were best when used on snow and ice.

△ DECORATED BOWS, used for harnessing pairs of horses.

AFTER THE ROMAN EMPIRE collapsed, Europe stagnated. Small states fought among themselves and the roads became neglected and overgrown. Wheeled transport all but disappeared. The most feared and adventurous travelers were the Viking raiders, who, in their magnificent longships, attacked swiftly from the sea. Their conquests ranged from Ireland to Russia and southwards to Italy. At home in Scandinavia, the best way of traveling was often by sleigh. Much of their country was impassable, and frozen lakes made the best highways. Experts felt that the Vikings were unlikely to have used wheels. But excavations at a royal Viking's burial site, at Oseberg, Norway, have since uncovered a horse-drawn wagon.

◁ THE FIRST SEA CONTAINER? The body of the Oseberg wagon, a waterproof tub, could be lifted from the wheeled chassis and lowered into a boat.

△ AT OSEBERG, an entire Viking ship and its contents, including a cart, had been buried in around A.D. 850. The tomb was sealed with a layer of clay which kept the wooden items intact until they were found in 1903. The cart and the removable container it carried were finely carved. The container was secured by means of ropes tied under the chins of the heads on the chassis frame.

MEDIEVAL EUROPE

△ A WINE-CART en route to a Norman ship before sailing the Channel to England.

IN THE ELEVENTH CENTURY, improvements in vehicles and animal power played a big part in developing trade throughout Europe. Padded horse-collars (allowing horses to pull heavier weights), iron horse-shoes and stirrups had appeared in Europe between A.D. 800 and 900. Iron-rimmed wheels followed, and four-wheeled vehicles were given swiveling front axles, allowing them to take sharper corners. In the fifteenth century passenger comfort improved when leather straps were used to suspend carriage bodies from the axle.

△ 14TH-CENTURY COACH with its body slung from its chassis.

Coaches hung like this probably first came from Holland.

△ THE SHELL in this pilgrim's hat denoted he had been to Santiago de Compostela.

◁ A LARGE WINE-CASK makes a heavy load for four men; a horse can pull as hard as 10 men.

△ A 1317 MANUSCRIPT about St. Denis of Paris showed the kinds of traffic that crossed the bridges over the Seine in a busy day.

▽ PEDESTRIANS and horse-riders used pedometers.

The old Roman highways were still used, but centuries of neglect had reduced them to rutted tracks. Broken wheels and upturned wagons were common. In some towns road maintenance was paid for by levying tolls, according to the size of vehicles. In the country, local rulers looked after the roads and unless there were special reasons for road repairs (such as a royal visit), they were not done.

△ DISTANCE RECORDER (odometer) devised by inventor Leonardo da Vinci (1452-1519).

◁ THE SCIENCE of distance-measuring made headway in the late Middle Ages. The Romans had used tapes or counted a marching soldier's pace. In the 16th century mechanized counters were introduced: pedometers for people or horses, odometers for vehicles.

△ DOESKIN SADDLE. Saddle- and harness-making became a very important craft as the use of horses increased.

Despite this gloomy picture of road travel, a lot of people set off on long trips. Many were pilgrims, visiting places as distant as Jerusalem in the Holy Land. Travel was slow - even royal messengers took a week to ride 400 miles, from Edinburgh to London. Inns were an essential part of traveling, for overnight stops and for changing horses. Stage wagons came into use in the fifteenth century; these slow vehicles, carrying goods or poor people, were so named because the inns where they paused formed the stages in their journey.

△ A WHIRLICOTE, a very early hackney carriage common in the 16th century.

▽ QUEEN ELIZABETH I's first coach arrived in England in 1565 and was made in Holland.

QUEEN ELIZABETH 1 (1533 1603) often rode a horse, in preference to riding in her coach.

△ ONE OF THE FIRST FIRE ENGINES. It was simply a water tank on wheels. It needed four men to pump out the water.

▽ STAGE WAGONS like this appeared in the 15th century. Six or more horses pulled it at walking pace. They were very uncomfortable - they had no springs and as many as 40 people were often crammed inside.

ANIMAL POWER

IT IS LIKELY that dogs, probably the first animals to be domesticated, were also the first to be used as draft animals. Early Eurasian nomads used their sled dogs for hunting reindeer (for food and hides), until it occurred to them that reindeers could pull sleds as well. But for hard traveling over long distances in the frozen wastes, dogs were generally favored because they could gulp down their meat in minutes, and get straight back to work, unlike vegetarian animals, who need much longer to chew and digest their food properly. The use of dogs for pulling carts was outlawed in England in 1837.

△ INDIAN ELEPHANTS in a ceremonial role: the Emperor of Delhi with his Indian and British officials, at a festival in 1813.

▽ NORTH AMERICAN INDIANS did not have horses until 1598 when Spanish settlers brought them to Santa Fe, New Mexico.

◁ ELEPHANTS AT WAR: although they tended to stampede, they made good shock troops. Armor was fitted, and swords were attached to sawn-off tusks.

▽ BULLOCK-CARTS are still to be seen in South-East Asia to the present day. These are hauling a ceremonial carriage.

▽ AN ASIAN DRAFT ANIMAL, the Bactrian camel, with a more humble burden.

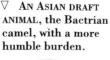

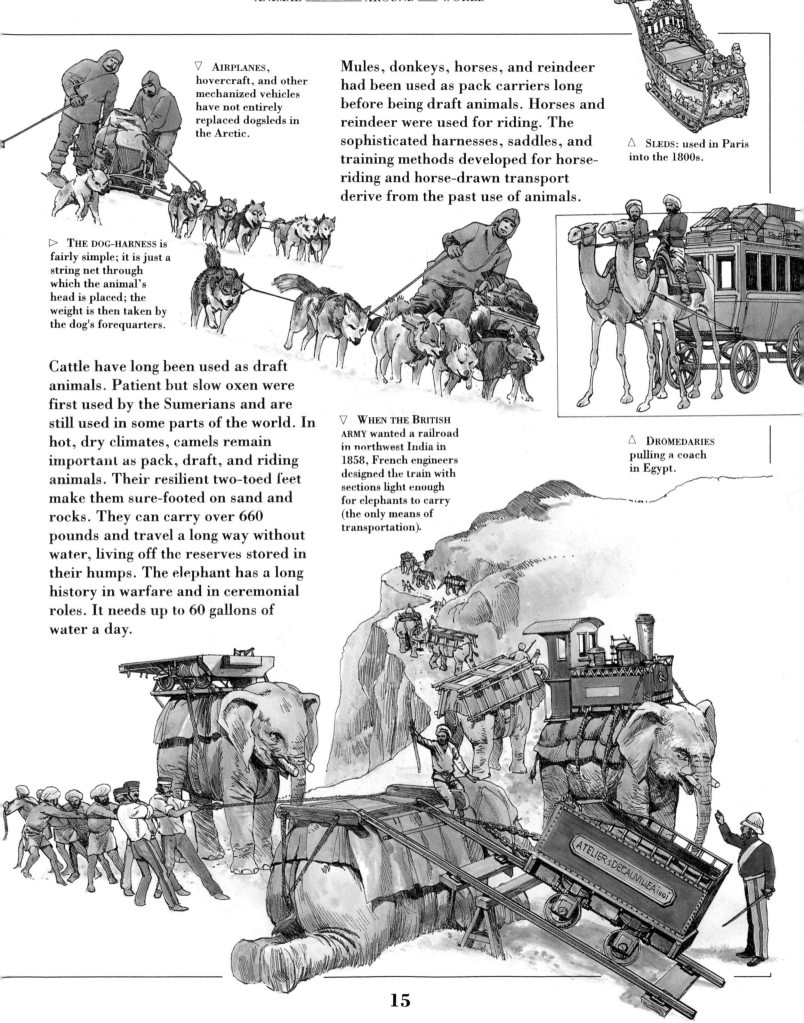

▽ AIRPLANES, hovercraft, and other mechanized vehicles have not entirely replaced dogsleds in the Arctic.

Mules, donkeys, horses, and reindeer had been used as pack carriers long before being draft animals. Horses and reindeer were used for riding. The sophisticated harnesses, saddles, and training methods developed for horse-riding and horse-drawn transport derive from the past use of animals.

△ SLEDS: used in Paris into the 1800s.

▷ THE DOG-HARNESS is fairly simple; it is just a string net through which the animal's head is placed; the weight is then taken by the dog's forequarters.

Cattle have long been used as draft animals. Patient but slow oxen were first used by the Sumerians and are still used in some parts of the world. In hot, dry climates, camels remain important as pack, draft, and riding animals. Their resilient two-toed feet make them sure-footed on sand and rocks. They can carry over 660 pounds and travel a long way without water, living off the reserves stored in their humps. The elephant has a long history in warfare and in ceremonial roles. It needs up to 60 gallons of water a day.

▽ WHEN THE BRITISH ARMY wanted a railroad in northwest India in 1858, French engineers designed the train with sections light enough for elephants to carry (the only means of transportation).

△ DROMEDARIES pulling a coach in Egypt.

15

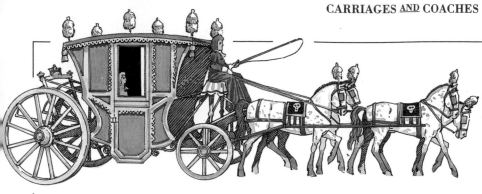

COACHES

◁ FRENCH FUNERAL COACH, 1600s. King Charles II (1630-85) demanded the English bring their coaches up to European standards.

▽ OLD STAGE WAGONS, traveling at 3 mph, often got in the way of faster, cheaper stagecoaches which could carry 40 people.

UNTIL 1700, THE FINEST COACHES had been made on the continent of Europe; but with rapid improvements in British technical knowledge and craftsmanship the center of excellence moved to England. There were better tools for woodworking, and iron and other metals were becoming more common. Plate-glass windows appeared just before 1700, and in 1787 John Collinge invented an axle that could hold oil for a month. Until then, daily oiling had been essential. In 1805, Obadiah Elliot devised elliptical carriage springs, which soon became universal. Before this, leather straps (see page 12) and crude C-shaped hangers had been the only protection against jolting. The Industrial Revolution that made these improvements possible, created extra transport; while canals carried the goods, people went by coach.

▷ STAGECOACHES carried between six and eight people, with their baggage on the roof.

A guard sat behind, with a Post Horn and a gun for scaring off highwaymen.

▽ THE TREND-SETTING BROUGHAM remained popular well into the 1900s. This type of carriage was first built in 1839 for a Lord Brougham. Its low-slung body made it easier to get in and out of. It is quite like the first motor cars.

BATH LONDON

Long-distance travel was by stagecoach. "Stages" were places where passengers could get on or off. Horses had to be changed every ten miles in order to keep up the speed. The most important coaches carried mail; in 1784 the London-to-Bath coach set a record average speed of 7 mph. By 1840, 22,000 miles of new roads had been built, with 800 turnpikes to collect tolls from users. Ways of keeping roads drained and smooth were devised by Scottish engineers Thomas Telford (1757-1834) and John McAdam (1756-1836).

△ THE FIRST LONDON OMNIBUS, introduced by George Shillibeer (1797-1866), ran in 1829. Later buses had seats on the top, with half-price fares for the passengers traveling in the open air. All buses were exclusively horse-drawn until the early 1900s.

▽ LIVERIED GROOM (*left*) and coachman, mid-19th century.

◁ GOING VISITING, 18th- century style. The sedan chair was just an adaptation of the litter from earlier times. For smart people, going about town like this avoided any risk of soiled clothes or contact with common people. Sedans could be hired, but rich people owned them.

△ THE PHAETON was popularized by the Prince of Wales in the 1790s. It was usually driven by its owner.

▽ AN 1850s AMERICAN ROCKAWAY, with some driver protection. The elliptical springs are clearly visible.

STEAM PIONEERS

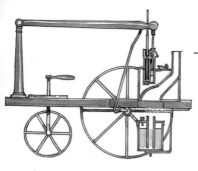

△ THIS 20-INCH LONG model steam carriage built by William Murdock ran for almost a mile in 1786.

△ PUFFING BILLY produced in 1813 by Christopher Blackett and William Hedley.

THE POWER OF STEAM was known in Greek times. In 130 B.C., the Greek Hero built a model engine in which jets of steam spun a shaft. In the 1770s many engineers built stationary steam engines powerful enough to drive machinery, and put them into factories, foundries, and mines. In the 1780s James Watt (1736-1819) made the first steam engines that were suitable to propel vehicles. He showed how a steam engine's sliding piston could drive a shaft or a wheel.

▽ THE LOCOMOTIVE *ROCKET*, built by George Stephenson, won the 1829 Rainhill trials in Britain.

In the 1500s, mines had wooden tracks for rolling wagons. Iron replaced wood in the 1700s and wagon wheels were given flanges to keep them on the rails. In 1804, Cornishman Richard Trevithick built a steam engine to run on rails - the first steam locomotive.

△ CUGNOT'S STEAM WAGON of 1770, used by the French army to haul heavy guns.

Cugnot's carriage had the boiler in front; fear of explosions put people off steam travel.

▽ GURNEY'S STEAM COACH ran between Gloucester and Cheltenham in 1831.

Stagecoachmen disliked Gurney's ideas and put him out of business.

△ STEPHENSON, who built the *Rocket*, sold steam engines abroad and often named them after the country they were going to.

LONDON AND BATH

ROYAL PATENT

NORTH AMERICA

△ THE PONY EXPRESS mail service only ran from 1860 to 1861. Electric telegraphs put it out of business.

A FTER 1830, unemployment and poverty drove many North Americans westward to seek their fortunes. Most of the migrants flooding west relied solely on animal power - until 1869, when the first coast-to-coast railroad opened.

△ THE WELLS FARGO COMPANY ran a 25-day mail coach service

from St. Louis to San Francisco; in 1869 trains took over.

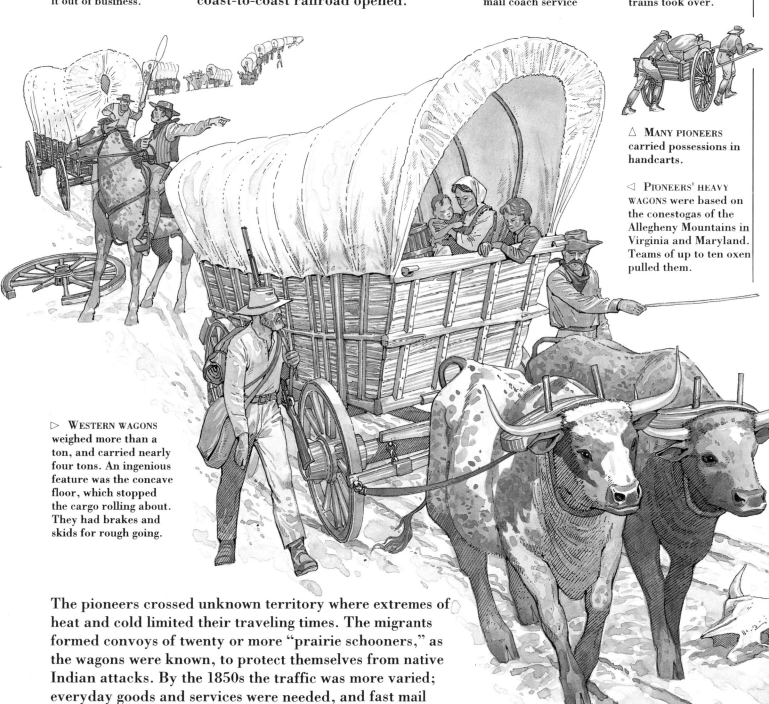

△ MANY PIONEERS carried possessions in handcarts.

◁ PIONEERS' HEAVY WAGONS were based on the conestogas of the Allegheny Mountains in Virginia and Maryland. Teams of up to ten oxen pulled them.

▷ WESTERN WAGONS weighed more than a ton, and carried nearly four tons. An ingenious feature was the concave floor, which stopped the cargo rolling about. They had brakes and skids for rough going.

The pioneers crossed unknown territory where extremes of heat and cold limited their traveling times. The migrants formed convoys of twenty or more "prairie schooners," as the wagons were known, to protect themselves from native Indian attacks. By the 1850s the traffic was more varied; everyday goods and services were needed, and fast mail services were established between settlements.

RAILROAD AGE

IRON RAILS HAD BIG ADVANTAGES. Wheels rolled so easily on rails that horses used to pull railroad wagons could manage loads ten times heavier than before. Passengers enjoyed greater comfort on horse-drawn streetcars - though still at a horse's pace. When steam engines replaced horses, passengers could travel without frequent stops and at seemingly terrifying speeds. Critics said that steam trains would kill plants and animals and, at such speeds, people would be unable to breathe.

△ *DEWITT CLINTON* (1831), the third steam engine in the U.S., ran from Albany and Schenectady at 20 mph. The train's carriages have outside seats like stagecoaches.

△ A HORSE-OPERATED treadmill locomotive, from 1831.

▽ STEPHENSON'S 1837 *North Star* broad-gauge engine.

△ THE *NORTH STAR* was made for the Great Western Railway.

△ BY 1869 ENGINES like this hauled the coast-to-coast trains across the U.S. Note the spark-arresting funnel (for pine forests and dry grasslands), the cowcatcher on the front, and the warning bell.

◁ 1843 MEDAL marks the opening of Belgium - Rhine rail link.

In 1825 the first public railroad opened between Stockton and Darlington, England. In the United States the Baltimore and Ohio, and Mohawk and Hudson railroads used steam after 1831. A railroad craze swept Europe and North America. But at first crashes were common.

△ *VULCAN* (named after the god of fire) ran on the Shrewsbury to Birmingham Railway in 1849.

◁ *VITTORIO EMANUELE II* from Italy first used 4-6-0 wheel layout.

By mid-century railroads were part of everyday life. Rail travel became acceptable to respectable people, once royalty and heads of state set the example. Railroad companies hired the finest engineers, and the locomotives and rolling stock became extremely refined; they worked well and looked good, too. Much of the technical knowledge came from Britain. Railroads soon spread into the remotest parts of Asia, Africa, and the Americas. Each country designed its railroad differently, to accommodate its own climate and terrain.

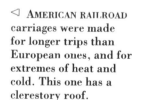

◁ AMERICAN RAILROAD carriages were made for longer trips than European ones, and for extremes of heat and cold. This one has a clerestory roof.

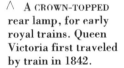

∧ A CROWN-TOPPED rear lamp, for early royal trains. Queen Victoria first traveled by train in 1842.

△ A NORWEGIAN TANK engine from the 1870s.

◁ AN ENGINE from the Tasmanian Government Railways, 1892. Both ran on tracks 3ft 6in apart.

Narrow-gauge railways are cheaper and use up less land. They can also be laid with tighter curves. They are used in places that have light traffic.

PEDAL POWER

△ THE PEDESTRIAN CURRICLE, a British velocipede with steering. Also known as the hobbyhorse.

IN PARIS IN THE 1790s, the two-wheel hobbyhorse was popular. In 1818, British and German makers added steering, which made the machines faster and safer. A fit rider could travel faster than a coach. In 1839 Kirkpatrick MacMillan, a Scottish blacksmith, made the first true bicycle by adding treadles, connected to the rear wheel. In the 1860s, the French firm Michaux built the original boneshaker with pedals driving the front wheels directly. The Rover "safety" bicycle of 1885 had pedals linked by a chain to the rear hub, almost like a modern bike. Pneumatic tires, invented by Dunlop in 1888, were soon common, and hub-mounted and Derailleur-type gears appeared around 1900. This set the scene for the modern bike.

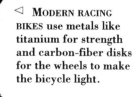

△ MACMILLAN'S 1839 invention was not ideal; it was hard for a seated rider to push the treadles to and fro.

△ THE CORRECT NAME of the 1870s penny-farthing was the ordinary bicycle.

Only the long-legged could ride it; others rode tricycles.

◁ A SOCIABLE OUTING on a tandem; the "safety" bicycle made the penny-farthing obsolete by 1885. Cycling became a fashionable pastime at the turn of the century.

▽ BY 1990 the most popular machine was the mountain bike.

It is specifically designed to cope with rough terrain.

◁ MODERN RACING BIKES use metals like titanium for strength and carbon-fiber disks for the wheels to make the bicycle light.

THE FIRST MOTORCYCLES

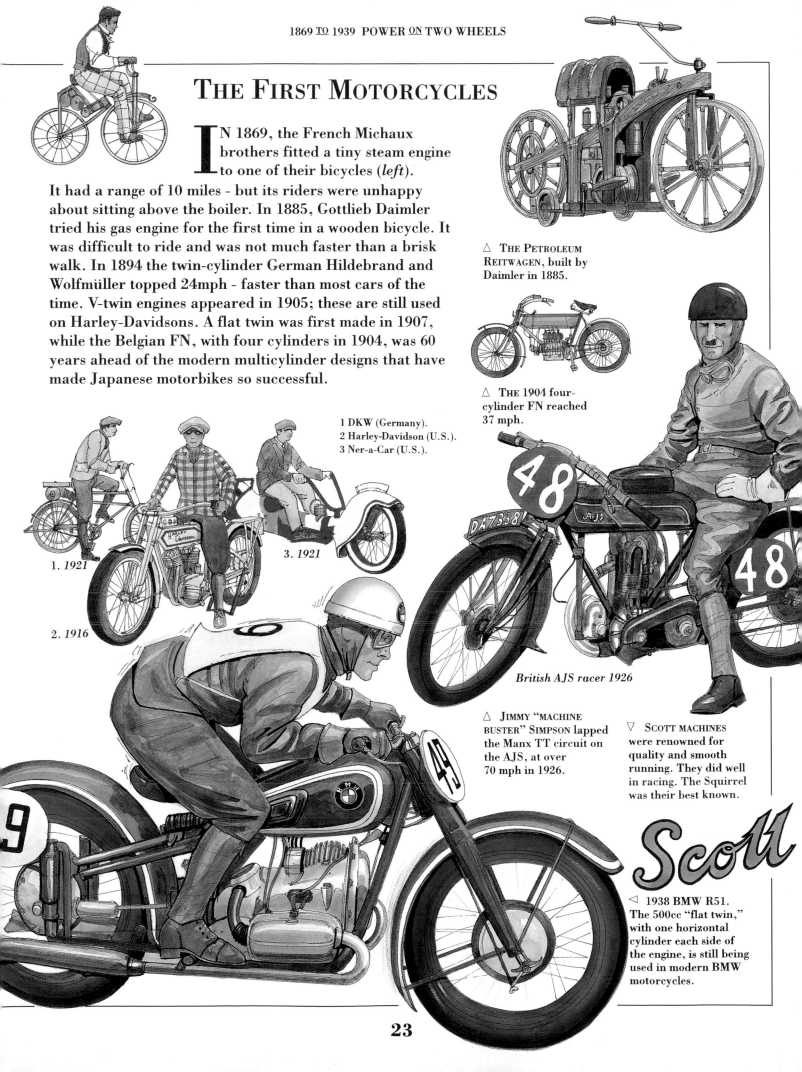

IN 1869, the French Michaux brothers fitted a tiny steam engine to one of their bicycles (*left*). It had a range of 10 miles - but its riders were unhappy about sitting above the boiler. In 1885, Gottlieb Daimler tried his gas engine for the first time in a wooden bicycle. It was difficult to ride and was not much faster than a brisk walk. In 1894 the twin-cylinder German Hildebrand and Wolfmüller topped 24mph - faster than most cars of the time. V-twin engines appeared in 1905; these are still used on Harley-Davidsons. A flat twin was first made in 1907, while the Belgian FN, with four cylinders in 1904, was 60 years ahead of the modern multicylinder designs that have made Japanese motorbikes so successful.

△ THE PETROLEUM REITWAGEN, built by Daimler in 1885.

△ THE 1904 four-cylinder FN reached 37 mph.

1 DKW (Germany).
2 Harley-Davidson (U.S.).
3 Ner-a-Car (U.S.).

1. 1921

2. 1916

3. 1921

British AJS racer 1926

△ JIMMY "MACHINE BUSTER" SIMPSON lapped the Manx TT circuit on the AJS, at over 70 mph in 1926.

▽ SCOTT MACHINES were renowned for quality and smooth running. They did well in racing. The Squirrel was their best known.

Scott

◁ 1938 BMW R51. The 500cc "flat twin," with one horizontal cylinder each side of the engine, is still being used in modern BMW motorcycles.

AUTOMOBILES

△ RICKETT'S 1858 three-wheel steamer.

▽ AMEDEE BOLLEE'S *l'Obeïssant* (the obedient one) steam carriage, 1873.

THE FIRST TRUE GAS-ENGINED CARS appeared in 1885. Two Germans, Carl Benz and Gottlieb Daimler, had developed internal combustion engines compact enough for road vehicles. Daimler's machine was a solid-looking carriage. Benz's version was a tricycle, using the new cycle technology. Cycle-makers at Peugeot attained the rights to use Daimler engines. Their success inspired Frenchmen René Panhard and Emile Levassor to make cars.

△ CARL BENZ'S 1885 three-wheel gas car went on trial in Mannheim , Germany.

◁ MOTORING created new fashions in clothing to protect against the weather and grime.

Battery- and steam-powered cars were attractive alternatives to noisy, smelly gas engines; they offered smooth and silent power, and were easier to drive. The internal combustion engine was rivaled on its way to popular use.

△ AN 1888 BENZ like this one was the first motor car to be brought to England.

△ 1895 PANHARD ET LEVASSOR; the car was slower with the hood up. The firm made tools for carpenters before making cars.

△ PEUGEOT PHAETON, 1894. A whip to chase off dogs was an option.

△ A PESSEY ELECTRIC CAR, 1897

▽ HENRY FORD (1863-1947, see p. 29) built his first car at home in Detroit in 1896.

The growth of motoring and car-building varied a great deal from country to country. Cars and the motoring industry were rapidly taken up in Germany and France, the French being particularly keen. They arranged many early trials and races. In England, the car was held back, literally, by a law of 1878 which restricted powered vehicles to walking pace; they were deemed to be so dangerous that they had to be led by a man carrying a red flag to warn pedestrians and horsemen ahead. In 1896, the law was repealed and the speed limit raised to 12 mph. This encouraged British firms, mostly established carriage- or cycle-makers, to build cars.

◁ BRITISH ELECTRIC CAR *l'Eléphant*, one of six electric entries in the 1898 Auto Club de France, Paris-Amsterdam race.

UNDERGROUND

THE WORLD'S FIRST SUBWAY was London's Metropolitan Railway in 1863. It was intended to link up the mainline stations (on the outskirts of the capital) and to carry passengers into the heart of London. The tunnels were not deep; they were brick-lined trenches covered with reinforced roofs, to support roads and buildings. Keeping the tunnels free from smoke and steam emitted by the engines was a problem.

△ A JUNCTION near London's Paddington station in 1863.

The tracks were for trains of 4 ft 8 in and 7ft in gauge.

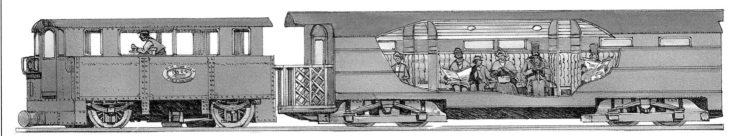

By 1890, electric trains were a reality. The first deep electric railway opened that year and linked London with the suburbs south of the River Thames. An engineer called J. H. Greathead had devised a tunneling shield; the men dug inside a tube which stopped the soft London clay falling in on them. As the shield advanced, tubular iron linings were placed in the tunnel - hence the Londoner's name for the subway: the tube. European cities, led by Budapest, and Paris in 1900, rapidly adopted transport beneath the city streets. New York opened its subway in 1904.

1 A Paris Metro train.
2 A Berlin train.
3 A stainless steel car on San Francisco's BART (Bay Area Rapid Transit) network.

Cities recognize the advantages of underground railways, though many of the older systems get overcrowded. In Tokyo (opened 1927) pushers are employed during the rush hour to squeeze people onto the trains.

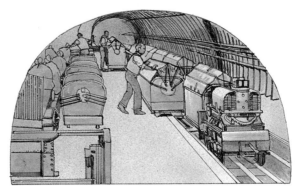

△ ORIGINAL ELECTRIC LOCOMOTIVE from the City & South London Railway, 1890.

The electricity was picked up from a third rail, between the running rails.

△ DRIVERLESS TRAINS on London's 6 mile Post Office

underground railway. One truck holds half a ton of mail.

Many subway trains are driverless. On London's Victoria line an operator controls the doors and starts the train. In Washington (opened 1976) the trains are controlled by a central computer system.

The "padded cell" carriages had no windows and held 96 passengers.

△ LONDON UNDERGROUND POSTERS were drawn by some of the best artists of the day. Alfred Leete drew this one in 1927, showing passengers being sucked towards the tube like dust to a vacuum cleaner.

▷ A CUTAWAY VIEW of London's Piccadilly Circus station in 1928, showing the warren of passages between the Piccadilly lines and the Bakerloo lines (102 ft and 86 ft) below the street.

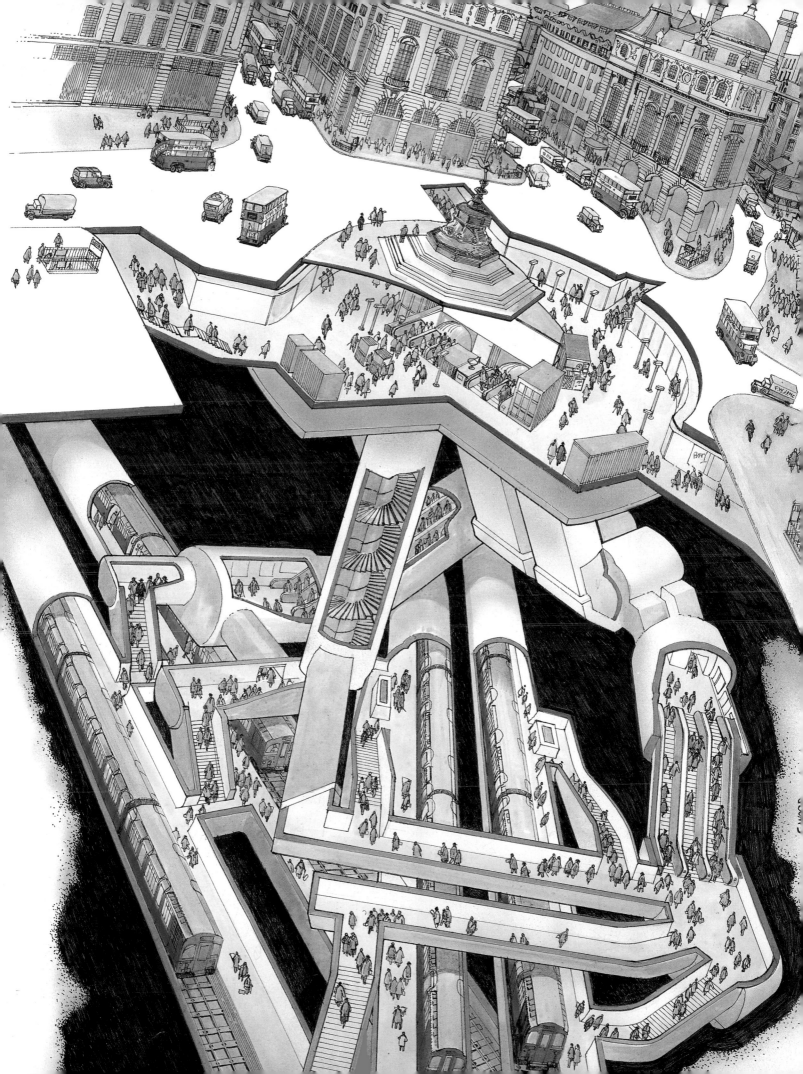

THE AUTOMOBILE

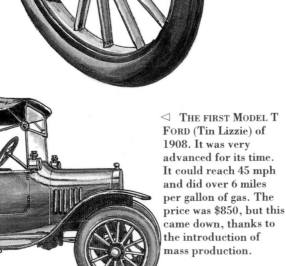

△ 1905 ROLLS-ROYCE. Royce, an engineer, and Rolls, a Panhard dealer, got together to build superior-quality motor cars.

IN 1900 THE FUTURE OF THE CAR WAS UNCLEAR. Steam was still seen as a useful alternative to gas, especially in America. But after 1912, when Cadillac brought out electric starters, no one wanted to wait several minutes for steam to be got up. In Europe there were "quality" cars and more modest products. Cheapest of all were the cycle-cars, using one- or two-cylinder motorcycle engines, with belts and pulleys to drive the wheels.

△ CARS GOT FASTER (and more drafty), so warmer clothes were needed. A goat skin coat worn by Chevalier René de Knytt.

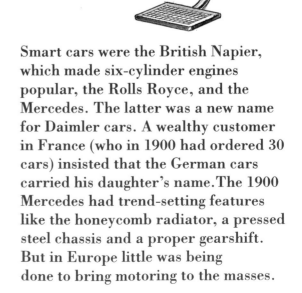

BOILER

◁ THE FIRST MODEL T FORD (Tin Lizzie) of 1908. It was very advanced for its time. It could reach 45 mph and did over 6 miles per gallon of gas. The price was $850, but this came down, thanks to the introduction of mass production.

Smart cars were the British Napier, which made six-cylinder engines popular, the Rolls Royce, and the Mercedes. The latter was a new name for Daimler cars. A wealthy customer in France (who in 1900 had ordered 30 cars) insisted that the German cars carried his daughter's name. The 1900 Mercedes had trend-setting features like the honeycomb radiator, a pressed steel chassis and a proper gearshift. But in Europe little was being done to bring motoring to the masses.

Henry Ford, who had built his own car in 1896 (see page 25), did more than anyone to make motoring popular. In 1911, he broke the monopoly of established American car-makers. He won a patent dispute with them, making his own products cheaper. In 1908 he introduced the famous Model T. The car was simplicity itself, intended for easy assembly and repair. Mass-production methods cut costs further. Driving the car was easy, too; its two-speed gearbox was worked by a single pedal. More than 15 million had been built when the last model rolled out in 1927.

△ BY 1925 A MODEL T cost $250. This was the final 1927 version.

CONDENSER

▽ THE 1903 WHITE STEAMER had a gas-fired boiler which was positioned under the seat. A radiator condensed steam from the engine, so that the water lasted longer.

▷ 1924 MODEL T. Driving this car was so easy with its pedal-controlled gears that some states issued lower-grade licences for Model T drivers.

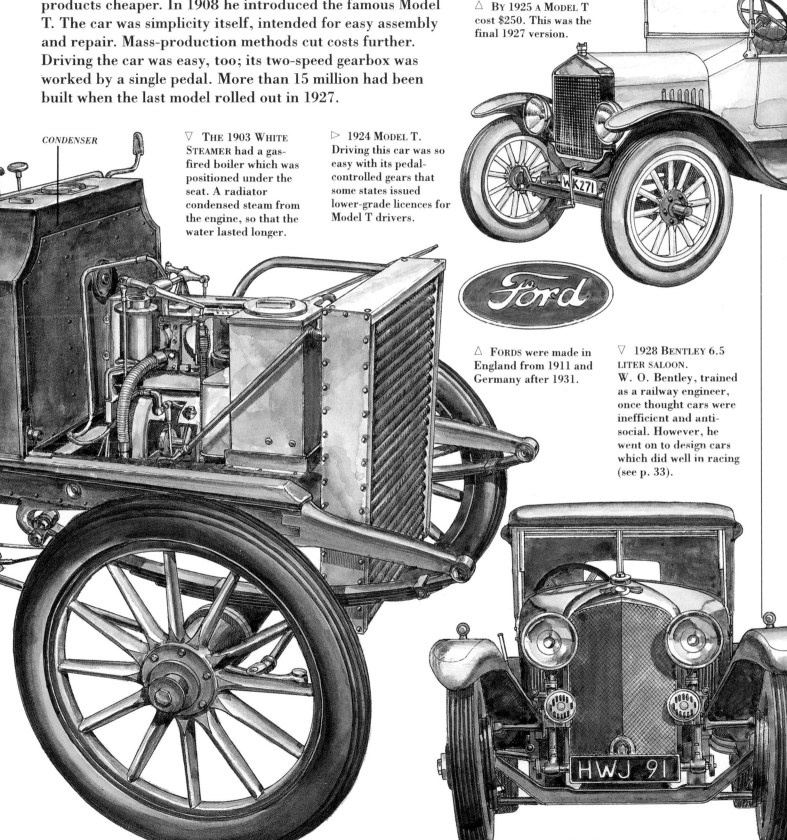

△ FORDS were made in England from 1911 and Germany after 1931.

▽ 1928 BENTLEY 6.5 LITER SALOON. W. O. Bentley, trained as a railway engineer, once thought cars were inefficient and anti-social. However, he went on to design cars which did well in racing (see p. 33).

STREETCARS

THE FIRST STREETCARS were in Harlem (1832) and New Orleans (1834). The smoothness of the rails meant that horses could haul more people - and at trotting speeds. Steam engines and horses were later ousted by electric power. The invention of the generator in the 1870s meant that electricity could be fed around towns by wires and cables.

△ A STEAM-DRIVEN HORSE- GROOMING MACHINE. Caring for horses was a major task for streetcar operators.

△ THIS CINCINNATI GRIP CAR, built in 1890, was hauled by a cable running back to a central engine shed.

▽ AFTER TOILING UPHILL, these two horses enjoyed a ride behind the streetcar in their caboose.

▷ THIS 1903 GLASGOW STREETCAR ran in 1959.

In 1881 the German engineer Ernst Werner von Siemens devised a safe overhead-wire system for supplying power to streetcars. But streetcars were threatened by underground railroads in larger cities. Motor buses were also catching on. More economical diesel engines and pneumatic tires made them even more popular by the 1930s. Twenty years later, streetcars had disappeared from many city streets.

▽ LONDON RT BUSES, 1939, had semi-automatic gearboxes.

▽ SINGLE-DECKER BUSES like this 1948 Daimler were common on country routes.

▷ ARTICULATED STREETCARS are common in Europe. These streetcars are in Bremerhaven, North Germany.

DELIVERIES

EARLY RAILROADS did little to improve the urban transport of goods. No railroad vehicle could carry deliveries to and from the doorstep, which is why railroad companies had (and still do have) fleets of vans and trucks. Towards the end of the last century, horse power was threatened by steam and gas engines. But the first gas-engined vans and trucks were noisy, used a lot of fuel, and often broke down. While steam engines were too heavy for cars, they could easily be put into larger vehicles. Their steady performance and smooth starting made them just right for the stop-start routine of deliveries. But it was the adoption of diesel engines in the 1930s that finally put an end to other forms of power in trucks, vans, and buses.

▽ DELIVERY WAGONS like these were used in towns up to 1930 by British railroads.

△ THIS BRITISH STEAM MAIL VAN was sold to Ceylon (now Sri Lanka) in 1901.

△ BREWERY DELIVERY VAN built in 1923 on a 30 horsepower Daimler car chassis. An ice-cream company built a van in the shape of a cone, with the driver peering through the "ice-cream."

▽ INTERNATIONAL K-series truck-tractor unit. It was built 1941-50 with an 8-ton capacity.

△ THE 1925 MORRIS-COMMERCIAL one-ton chassis cost £172. The customer built his own body onto it.

▽ AN OPEL-BLITZ "lightning" truck from Germany. This three-tonner appeared in the early 1930s. The same model appeared as a four-wheel-drive army truck, and as a fire engine in the 1950s.

RACING CARS

T HE FIRST MOTOR RACE was held in France in 1895. On his own, Emile Levassor drove from Paris to Bordeaux and back, nearly 750 miles in 48 hours. He won simply because his car did not break down. A Peugeot came in second, nearly six hours later. A racing craze swept France and the rest of Europe. The contests were held on public roads, and spectators were often injured. Huge engines, many over three gallons, were used. To make the contests fairer, formulas were introduced. These laid down sizes and weights for the car-makers. Under a 1902 rule, cars had to weigh less than one ton. In 1906, the first Grand Prix was held under this formula.

△ BOILLOT won the 1912 French Grand Prix in a Peugeot. Its

2 gallon engine rotated much faster than earlier ones.

△ BUGATTI-TYPE 35, 1924. It had an 8-cylinder "in line" engine. In 1926 a supercharger was added to produce extra power.

△ THE ALFA ROMEO 158 won three Grand Prix races in 1950.

△ STIRLING MOSS rose to fame in 1957 in the Maserati 250F.

△ THE TINY 1963 LOTUS-CLIMAX 25 was driven by Jim Clark.

△ A LOTUS 72 made Fittipaldi world champion in 1972.

△ THE 1975 AND 1979 FERRARIS look similar, but the later car has

"skirts" to suck it down onto the track to give it more grip.

LOTUS

Ferrari

△ LOTUS AND FERRARI make road cars as well as racers. The founders Colin Chapman and Enzo Ferrari both raced as young men.

◁ AYRTON SENNA at a pit stop in his 1990 MP4/5B. Tire changes can take eight seconds or even less.

◁ BENTLEYS WON AT LE MANS five times from 1924 to 1930.

▽ THE FRENCH TOWN LE MANS is steeped in motoring history. In 1873, Bollée (see p. 24) experimented with his steam car there. 1923 saw the first 24-hour race, an annual prestige match between the world's sports car makers.

▽ THE MULSANNE STRAIGHT on the Le Mans route is the longest and fastest anywhere.

Mulsanne

Tetre Rouge

Hanaudières

Amage

White house

JAGUAR D-TYPE, 1955 Le Mans winner.

FORD GT40, four times victor, 1966 to 1969.

PORSCHE 917, 1970 winner.

MERCEDES, winners in 1989.

△ A CAVALCADE of Le Mans winners shows how the cars have developed from road-legal sports cars to streamlined projectiles.

Until 1933 names like *Muserati*, *Alfa Romeo*, and *Bugatti* dominated the major races. British makes like Bentley and Sunbeam occasionally won. But from 1934 until 1939 the new German Mercedes-Benz and Auto-Union cars dominated Grand Prix races. These cars could reach nearly 200 mph, as fast as a modern Formula 1 car. In the 1960s all cars became rear-engined, tires became wider and airfoils were used to press the cars down onto the track at speed. As a result, they could take corners at very high speeds. Racing has often been criticized for being risky. But many features now common in family cars - disk brakes, fuel injection, and turbochargers - were first tried out on the racetrack.

RAILROADS

△ NORTH SCOTTISH RAILWAY *Gordon Highlander*, 1900.

▷ THE BRITISH *MALLARD* reached 126 mph in 1938.

FOR THE FIRST HALF of the twentieth century the railroads remained the most important means of transportation. The 1930s and 1940s saw the fastest and largest steam locomotives ever built. But steam was to be challenged by more efficient forms of power.

△ ENGINES like this hauled trains from London to Scotland and regularly ran at 100 mph.

Fast engines used the 4-6-2 *Pacific* wheel layout. 6ft 3in driving wheels were common.

▽ HEAT from the firebox passes to the smokebox through the boiler tubes, heating the water.

Cutaway of 1950s PACIFIC locomotive.

Steam engines produced too much pollution. They needed the skills of a driver and a stoker or fireman. They also needed to take on water and coal at regular intervals. Diesel locomotives were favored on America's long-distance routes; they could keep going on a tank of fuel. Electric locomotives were good for busy routes and in places with cheap electricity. Both types produced no soot or grime, and started at the turn of a switch.

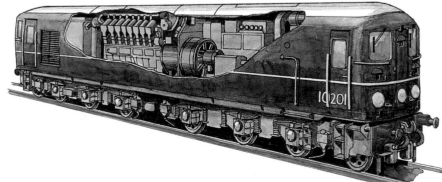

Pantograph

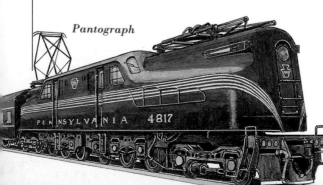

◁ AN AMERICAN 7,500 ELECTRIC LOCOMOTIVE, from 1934. The pantograph current pick-up can be folded away when not in use.

△ DIESEL-ELECTRICS have no gearbox like a car; the train engine drives a generator which feeds electric motors on the axles.

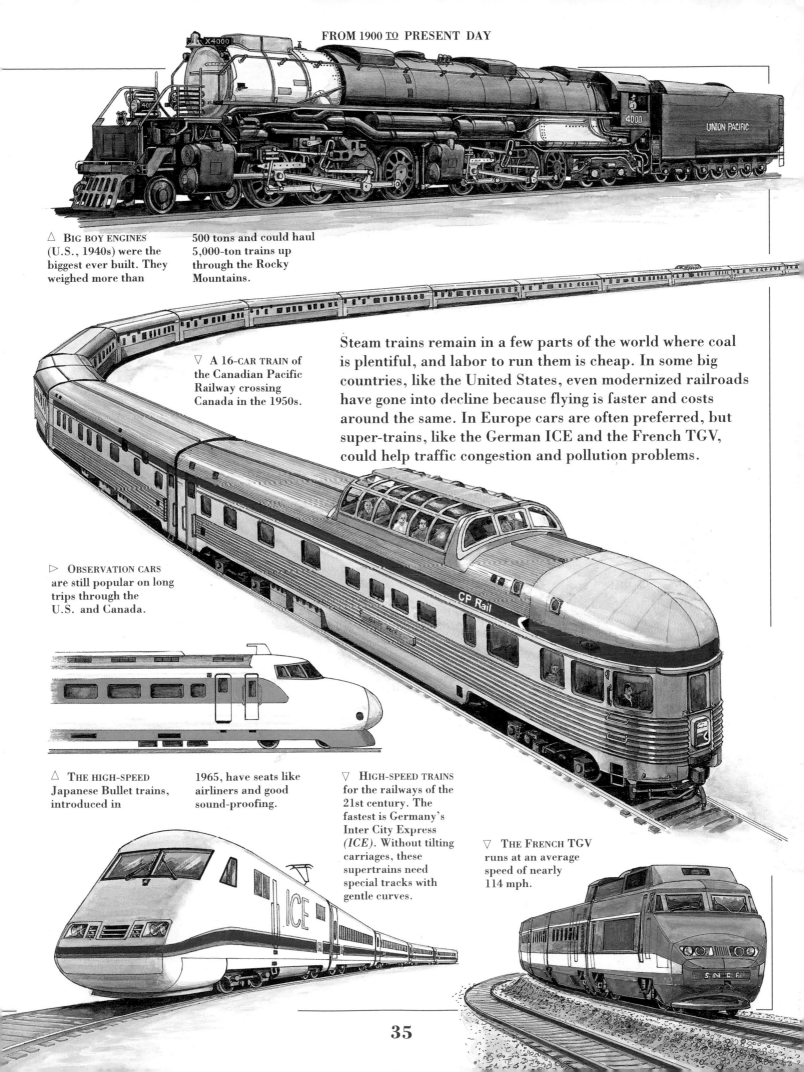

△ BIG BOY ENGINES (U.S., 1940s) were the biggest ever built. They weighed more than 500 tons and could haul 5,000-ton trains up through the Rocky Mountains.

▽ A 16-CAR TRAIN of the Canadian Pacific Railway crossing Canada in the 1950s.

Steam trains remain in a few parts of the world where coal is plentiful, and labor to run them is cheap. In some big countries, like the United States, even modernized railroads have gone into decline because flying is faster and costs around the same. In Europe cars are often preferred, but super-trains, like the German ICE and the French TGV, could help traffic congestion and pollution problems.

▷ OBSERVATION CARS are still popular on long trips through the U.S. and Canada.

△ THE HIGH-SPEED Japanese Bullet trains, introduced in 1965, have seats like airliners and good sound-proofing.

▽ HIGH-SPEED TRAINS for the railways of the 21st century. The fastest is Germany's Inter City Express (ICE). Without tilting carriages, these supertrains need special tracks with gentle curves.

▽ THE FRENCH TGV runs at an average speed of nearly 114 mph.

MOTORCYCLES

IMMEDIATELY AFTER 1945 motorcycles, some with sidecars, were an important way of travel in Europe. But most were noisy, unreliable machines. Then Europe was taken by surprise by an invasion of Japanese machines. In 1945 there were fewer than 2,000 motorcycles in Japan, compared with the half-million built in Germany in 1938. But the Honda company had studied European cycles and sold five mopeds to England, in 1957. By 1969 they had sold nearly a million motorcycles. In 1960 the Honda two-cylinder 250cc Dream offered 95 mph - a speed reached only by much more expensive European machines. Other Japanese cycle-makers followed Honda's lead. They also dominated racing. With widespread car ownership since the 1970s, motorcycles belong mostly to enthusiasts.

▽ MOTORCYCLES for popular off-road events use knobbly tires and supple suspension. This BMW was in the 1985 Paris-Dakar rally.

△ BMW WITH SIDECAR in use by the German army, World War II.

▽ HARLEY-DAVIDSON - one of the few makes to survive Japanese competition. Despite being based on old designs, they cruise well and are reliable.

△
▷ HIGHWAY PATROLS, Hell's Angels, Easy Riders - big Harleys handle them all.

▽ KENNY ROBERTS and the Yamaha YZR500 - the names to beat in Grand Prix racing between 1978 and 1980.

▽ MANY SUPERBIKES now use racing technology: alloy wheels and frames and "high-revving" engines.

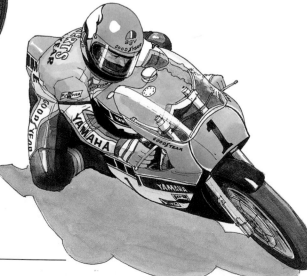

ROAD HAULAGE

INCREASING A TRUCK'S LOAD has always been a concern for designers. Steam wagons, used mainly in England, were limited by the weight of the engine, coal, and water. The Thorneycroft Company, in London, had an ingenious way of solving this; they built a four-wheel tractor to pull a 4-ton load behind it on a flat two-wheel trailer. This was the first articulated truck. In the United States gas-engined trucks were more common. In World War I the Allied armies used vast fleets of motor trucks. In Europe, more economical diesel engines were adopted in the 1930s. The Americans took to them later. Turbocharged diesel engines are now almost universally used in trucks.

△ FODEN-BUILT STEAM WAGONS from 1900 to 1931; a 1912 model. Note the small space for the 4-ton load.

▽ LEYLAND 3-TON TRUCK, World War II.

▷ HIGHWAY BUILDING and opencast mining need maximum load capacity, which was provided by this huge off-road Terex 33 -11B earth-mover.

◁ THE MACK COMPANY, founded in 1902, is one of the U.S.'s biggest heavy truck-makers. One model had an 800 horsepower V16 engine.

▽ MARMON TRUCKS date back to 1902. This is a typical American long-haul tractor. The cab is set back away from the engine. Behind it is a rest cabin for the driver.

MODERN CARS

△ 1933 CADILLAC PHAETON (see p. 17); body by Fleetwood, 1.5 gallon V12 engine.

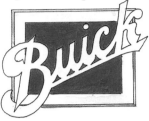

△ THE CITROEN 2CV - a challenging and popular design from 1949; it stayed in production up to 1989.

BENEATH THE BODYWORK, most cars of the mid-1930s used Panhard's layout of the 1890s: engine at the front, gearbox in the middle, and rear-wheel drive. Frenchman André Citroën challenged this. His famous Light 15 of 1934 had front-wheel drive. This left more space for passengers and baggage. Dr Ferdinand Porsche's 1936 rear-wheel drive Volkswagen had an engine-gearbox unit squeezed right to the rear of the car. Both these car bodies were so strong that a separate chassis was not necessary; the suspension and power unit were attached directly to the body. Curved pressed-steel panels were used, welded together into a monocoque shell.

△ 1940 PACKARD "SUPER EIGHT" CONVERTIBLE, with 160 hp, 8-cylinder engine.

△ THE BUICK MOTOR CAR CO., Michigan, was founded in 1903. It was a founder-member of General Motors, 1908.

▽ ALEC ISSIGONIS' 1949 MORRIS MINOR. With only a few changes, Morris Minor production lasted until 1970. Over a million had been built by 1961.

After World War II cars did not alter much. An exception was the 1948 Morris Minor, the work of the British engineer Alec Issigonis. Ten years later he designed the Mini, a tiny car with big-car performance. Its success was due to its revolutionary transverse engine-gearbox unit at the front of the car. Over thirty years later almost every car built has this layout.

MWB 816

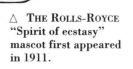

△ THE ROLLS-ROYCE "Spirit of ecstasy" mascot first appeared in 1911.

△ RILEY 1.5 LITRE RME SALOON, 1953.

The Riley company was started in 1898.

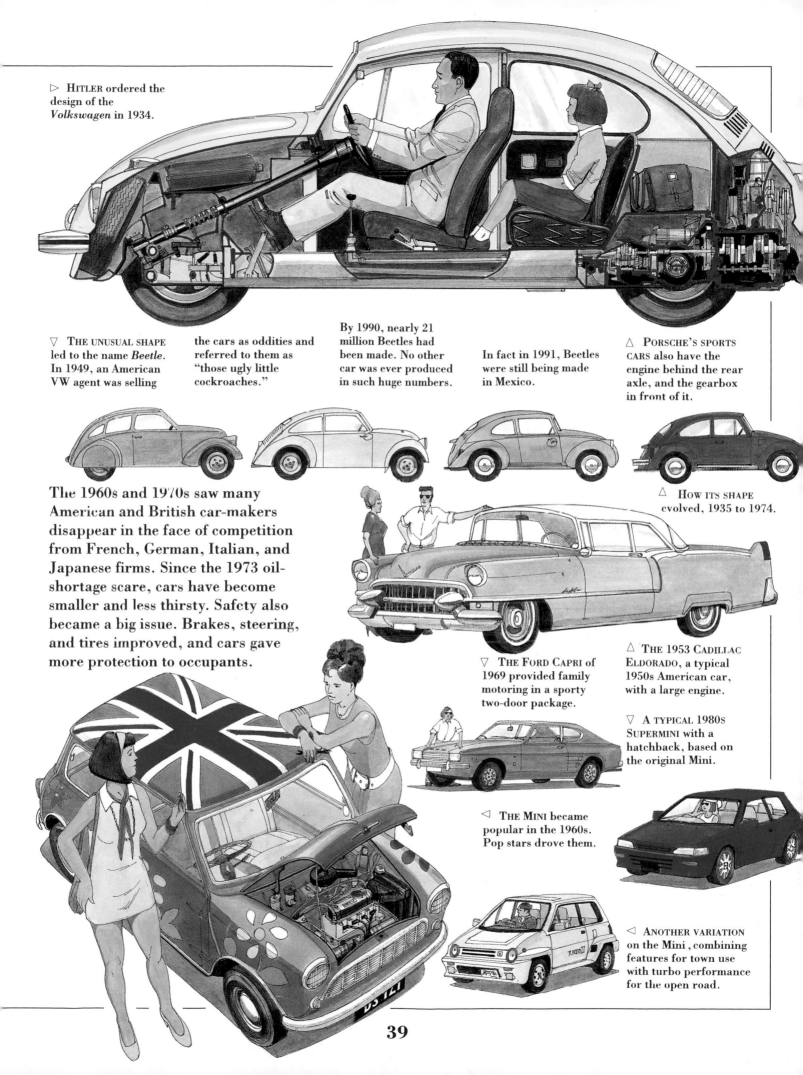

▷ HITLER ordered the design of the *Volkswagen* in 1934.

▽ THE UNUSUAL SHAPE led to the name *Beetle*. In 1949, an American VW agent was selling the cars as oddities and referred to them as "those ugly little cockroaches."

By 1990, nearly 21 million Beetles had been made. No other car was ever produced in such huge numbers.

In fact in 1991, Beetles were still being made in Mexico.

△ PORSCHE'S SPORTS CARS also have the engine behind the rear axle, and the gearbox in front of it.

△ HOW ITS SHAPE evolved, 1935 to 1974.

The 1960s and 1970s saw many American and British car-makers disappear in the face of competition from French, German, Italian, and Japanese firms. Since the 1973 oil-shortage scare, cars have become smaller and less thirsty. Safety also became a big issue. Brakes, steering, and tires improved, and cars gave more protection to occupants.

▽ THE FORD CAPRI of 1969 provided family motoring in a sporty two-door package.

△ THE 1953 CADILLAC ELDORADO, a typical 1950s American car, with a large engine.

▽ A TYPICAL 1980s SUPERMINI with a hatchback, based on the original Mini.

◁ THE MINI became popular in the 1960s. Pop stars drove them.

◁ ANOTHER VARIATION on the Mini, combining features for town use with turbo performance for the open road.

39

PRODUCTION

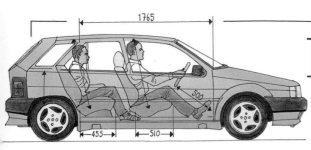

△ SEDANS are laid out to make the best possible use of interior space.

△ ONLY ESSENTIAL REAR-VIEW MIRRORS interrupt the sedan's carefully designed smooth outline.

△ REAR VIEW of a sedan showing how even the exhaust is tucked underneath out of the airstream.

STYLING, value for money, interior space and comfort, safety, low running costs, and performance are all features that potential car buyers look for. Years before a new car goes into production, a car-maker's market research experts will have gathered opinions from a wide range of owners of similar cars of other makes. They learn what people like and dislike about their cars and what they would like to see in a new model. They also test the competing cars to get first-hand knowledge of their strengths and weaknesses. Their findings then go to the styling and engineering experts, and a clay model is built to give a clear idea of how the new car will look. At this early stage, precise details of the car's outlines are fed into a CAD (computer-aided design) system, to provide a data base which will eventually be translated into hard facts for the engineers who have to manufacture all the parts and program the assembly-plant robots.

△ THE COMPUTER allows the effects of design changes to be easily predicted.

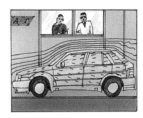

△ IN THE WIND TUNNEL, tapes on the scale model show the airflow around the car.

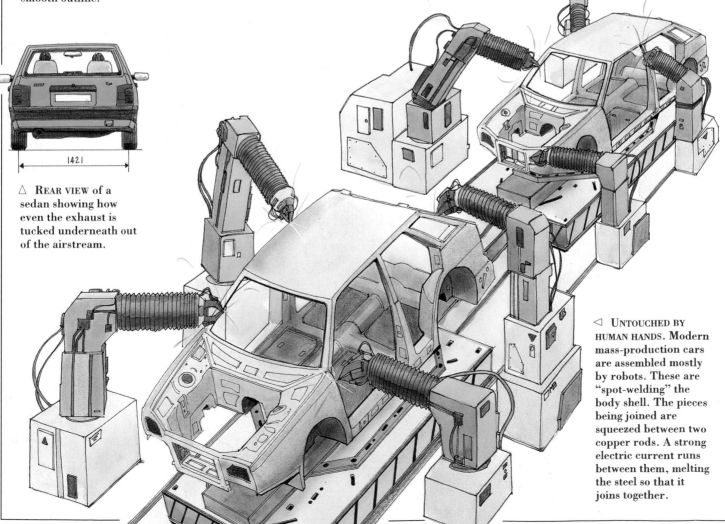

◁ UNTOUCHED BY HUMAN HANDS. Modern mass-production cars are assembled mostly by robots. These are "spot-welding" the body shell. The pieces being joined are squeezed between two copper rods. A strong electric current runs between them, melting the steel so that it joins together.

△ AT THE EARLIEST STAGES of design, sketches and scale models are made.

△ WHEN THE BASIC CONCEPT is accepted, a full-size model is built in clay.

This is often painted to look like a real car so that opinions can be sought at this stage.

The final product is a blend of styling and engineering. The car needs to be strong and light, and yet look good, and the body panels must be cheap to make and to replace after bumps. Wind resistance uses up fuel, so a car's shape has to have a low CD (drag coefficient). Demands for environment-friendlier cars mean fuel economy and low exhaust emissions; these limit speed and acceleration. The maker has to get this right the first time. The cost of producing a million cars does not allow for mistakes.

△ CONSULTANTS and marketing experts look at the model to make sure that it is going to be a success.

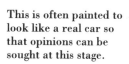

△ THE DASHBOARD is the most complex assembly in a modern car, apart from the engine.

▷ THE COMPLETED BODY SHELL is fitted onto a unit consisting of the engine-gearbox assembly and the front suspension. Final testing is done automatically in the factory - the car is not driven before delivery.

▷ TWO-LITER 16 VALVE Fiat tipo engine.

FUTURE

CROWDED PARTS of the world face big transportation problems. Road vehicles offer personal freedom and door-to-door travel; yet they cause unacceptable congestion and pollution. Present-day exhaust emission controls, lead-free gas, and electric car trials are only minor solutions to a growing problem.

▷ THE ULTIMATE HIGH-SPEED TRAINS will use Maglev. The train hovers over magnetic coils which also propel it. In a transparent tunnel, speeds of over 430 mph could be reached with safety.

▷ A SOLAR-POWERED CAR has already been demonstrated.

AFTER DARK there isn't much solar power. It may become possible to take your electric car or city bike to a solar recharging station.

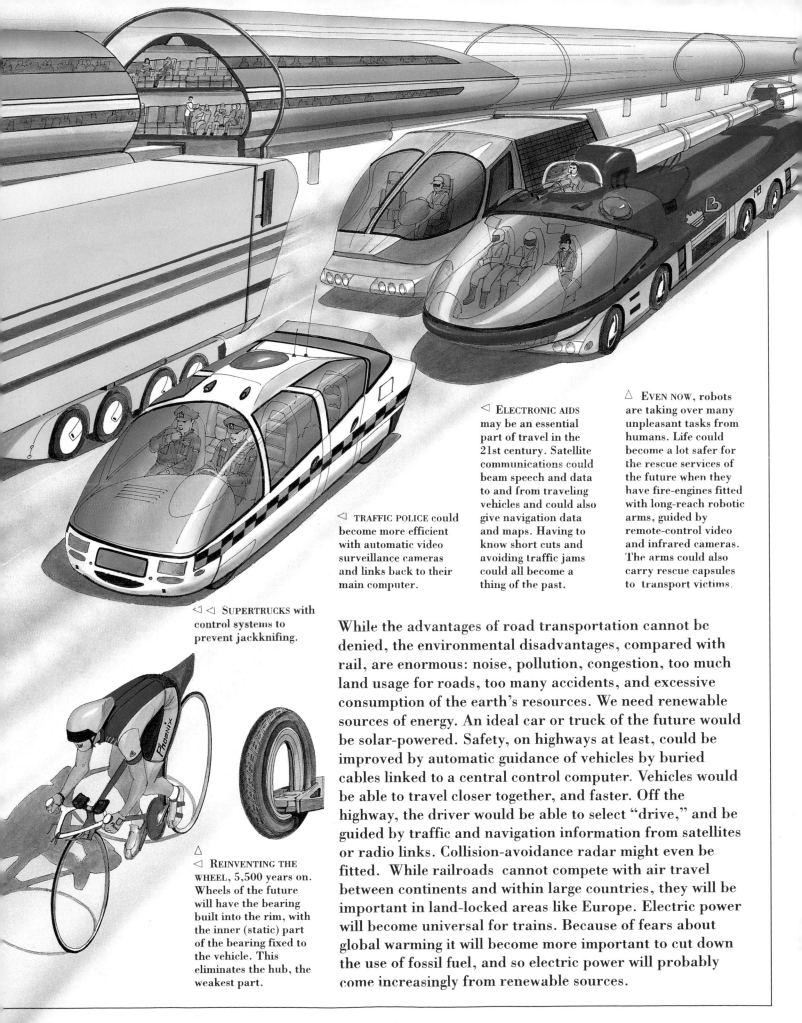

◁ ELECTRONIC AIDS
may be an essential
part of travel in the
21st century. Satellite
communications could
beam speech and data
to and from traveling
vehicles and could also
give navigation data
and maps. Having to
know short cuts and
avoiding traffic jams
could all become a
thing of the past.

△ EVEN NOW, robots
are taking over many
unpleasant tasks from
humans. Life could
become a lot safer for
the rescue services of
the future when they
have fire-engines fitted
with long-reach robotic
arms, guided by
remote-control video
and infrared cameras.
The arms could also
carry rescue capsules
to transport victims.

◁ TRAFFIC POLICE could
become more efficient
with automatic video
surveillance cameras
and links back to their
main computer.

◁ ◁ SUPERTRUCKS with
control systems to
prevent jackknifing.

△
◁ REINVENTING THE
WHEEL, 5,500 years on.
Wheels of the future
will have the bearing
built into the rim, with
the inner (static) part
of the bearing fixed to
the vehicle. This
eliminates the hub, the
weakest part.

While the advantages of road transportation cannot be
denied, the environmental disadvantages, compared with
rail, are enormous: noise, pollution, congestion, too much
land usage for roads, too many accidents, and excessive
consumption of the earth's resources. We need renewable
sources of energy. An ideal car or truck of the future would
be solar-powered. Safety, on highways at least, could be
improved by automatic guidance of vehicles by buried
cables linked to a central control computer. Vehicles would
be able to travel closer together, and faster. Off the
highway, the driver would be able to select "drive," and be
guided by traffic and navigation information from satellites
or radio links. Collision-avoidance radar might even be
fitted. While railroads cannot compete with air travel
between continents and within large countries, they will be
important in land-locked areas like Europe. Electric power
will become universal for trains. Because of fears about
global warming it will become more important to cut down
the use of fossil fuel, and so electric power will probably
come increasingly from renewable sources.

Sumerian chariots

TIMELINE

Pony Express

B.C.
c.3500 Wheels used for making pottery in Sumeria for the first time; wheels used on carts and wagons about the same time.
c.2000 Four-wheel carts used in Crete.
c.1600 Hyksos bring the idea of two-wheel chariots to Egypt.
c.1300 Egyptians repel Hittite invaders with improved chariots.

Decorations from a chariot, 1420 B.C.

c.1000 Chariots appear in Greece.
c.1000 - 200 Road and canal network built in China.
312 The Appian Way is built by the Roman censor Caecus.

Elephants at war

130 Hero, in Greece, makes a rotating machine which is driven by steam .
c.130 Roman roads extend over Europe and the middle East.
A.D.
c.850 Padded horse-collars introduced to Europe, making horses many times more effective.
c.1400 Coach bodies hung from leather straps, making for greater comfort.
c.1500 Distance meter (odometer) invented by Leonardo da Vinci.

Charioteer from the tomb of Qin Shih Hwang-ti

c.1550 The first wooden tracks for guiding mine and quarry trucks appear. Windowless and unsprung stage wagons provide public transport in England.
1598 Spanish settlers in New Mexico introduce horses to American Indians.

c.1650 Faster stage coaches in England.
1700 Plate-glass windows fitted in coaches.
1712 Thomas Newcomen invents a steam engine for pumping water.
1770 In France, Joseph Cugnot builds a steam wagon for hauling guns.

French funeral coach

1780-81 James Watt builds "rotative" engines - a vital step towards steam-powered vehicles.
1784 First mail coach service runs between London and Bath.
1786 Murdock, an engineer, builds a model steam tricycle carriage.
1787 Collinge's self-oiling axle for coaches invented.
1794 Ball bearing invented.
Early 1800s Several experiments with "explosion engines" - forerunners of the internal combustion engine.
1804 Cornishman Richard Trevithick builds the first self-propelled steam engine to run on rails.
1805 Obadiah Elliot invents elliptical steel strings, improving comfort in coaches.

Steam locomotive

1818 Front-wheel steering added to two-wheeled hobbyhorses.
1825 First public railway, linking Stockton with Darlington, opens in England.
First omnibus service starts in Paris.
1829 Shillibeer's omnibus introduced in London.

1829 The *Rocket* built by George Stephenson wins the Rainhill trials for the finest steam locomotive.
1830 First time for mail to be carried by train, between Liverpool and Manchester.
1831 In the U.S., Baltimore and Ohio, and Mohawk and Hudson railways use steam engines. Goldsworthy Gurney introduces his steam carriage service in the west of England.
1832 The first horse-drawn streetcar service opens in Harlem, New York.
1834 New Orleans horse-drawn streetcar service opens.
1837 Dog-hauled carts banned by law in England.
1839 The Brougham carriage first appears, setting a standard for all others.
1839 Kirkpatrick MacMillan, a Scottish blacksmith, invents a bicycle with pedals.
c.1840 Migration of pioneers, in western wagons, to the far west of the U.S. starts.

1841 Sir Charles Wheatstone builds a linear motor, the sort of motor to be used for "Maglev" trains.
1842 Queen Victoria's first train journey.
1844 Wells Fargo express mail coach service starts to serve the western settlements.
1845 John McAdam's road-making process improved by adding tar to bind the surface gravel together.
1860 Static gas engine perfected in France. The Pony Express mail service starts in the U.S.
1861 The Pony Express is put out of business by the electric telegraph.

Pedestrian Curricle

1863 London's Metropolitan Railway is the world's first underground.
1869 Coast-to-coast railroad across the USA opens. The popularity of the new railroad system marked the gradual collapse of stage coaches as a means of transport. In France, the Michaux brothers build the first practical steam-powered bicycle. It can travel 10 miles. But the boiler under the seat worries riders of the bike.
1876 Otto and Langen produce the Otto "silent" engine, the forerunner of the type of engine to be used in automobiles.

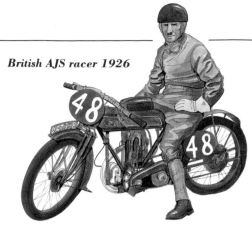

British AJS racer 1926

1881 In Germany, Werner von Siemens devises the overhead-wire method of feeding electricity to streetcars or electric trains.
1885 The Rover "safety" bicycle soon makes the penny-farthing obsolete. The first gas-engined vehicle is built - Gottlieb Daimler's wooden motorcycle. It can reach up to 7 mph but it is difficult to ride. Carl Benz's gas-engined tricycle uses a two-cycle, one-cylinder engine.

Metropolitan Railway in 1863

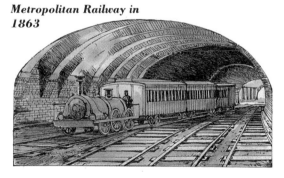

1885 Daimler makes a four-wheeled, gas-driven car.
1888 Dunlop invents the pneumatic tire, first used on bicycles.
1890 First true "tube" railway (in a deep tunnel) linking the City and south London is opened in England.
1895 Paris-Bordeaux motor race held. The winner takes 48 hours.
1896 In England, the automobile no longer has to be driven at walking pace. The speed limit was raised to 12 mph.

1896 Henry Ford builds his first car in Detroit. The start of a transportation revolution.
1900 The Paris Metro opens in France. The name *Mercedes* is first used on Daimler cars after a rich Frenchman orders 30 cars and demands that the cars carry his daughter's own name.
1902 Dr F. Lanchester invents disk brakes, a similar idea to bicycle brake pads.
1904 New York's underground railway, the "subway," opens.

1905 Rolls-Royce is established. Their first car is nicknamed the "silver ghost" because it is so quiet and has a recognizable, shining aluminum body.
1908 Henry Ford introduces his Model T, a simple easy-to-drive car, and works towards bringing motoring to the masses.

1905 Rolls-Royce

1913 Gasoline supplies boosted (a shortage has threatened development of the car) by William M. Burton's invention of the "cracking" process to extract gas from crude oil.
1923 The first Le Mans 24-hour motor race is held in France. It is held on public roads and many spectators are injured.

1927 The production of the Ford Model T stops. More than 15 million models of this hugely popular car have rolled off the production line.
1934 André Citroën introduces the "traction avant" Light 15 car which has front-wheel drive.

Volkswagen "Beetle"

1936 The first Volkswagen (car for the people) appears, with a rear-mounted engine. It is designed by Ferdinand Porsche and commissioned by Hitler. The car's shape earns it the nickname *Beetle*. The original design changes very little up to 1990.
1938 *Mallard* reaches 126 mph while pulling a seven-coach train - a record for steam locomotives.

1941 The American Big Boy steam locomotives appear. They are the heaviest locomotives built, and weigh over 500 tons.
1948 The Morris Minor car appears, designed by Alec Issigonis. Eric Laithwaite builds his first linear electric motor.
1958 The Mini (again, by Issigonis) is the first car to have a combined front engine and gearbox across the chassis.

Gordon Highlander 1900

1960 Last British steam locomotive built.
1962 The Moulton bicycle has a frame that can fit anyone and carry heavy weights. The American car industry, in its 66th year, makes its 200 millionth automobile.

1964 Donald Campbell in the *Bluebird* reaches 403 mph - a world record for cars with driven wheels (as distinct from jet cars).
1965 An American lawyer Ralph Nader publishes a book called *Unsafe at Any Speed*, which makes car-makers think about making cars safer.
1967 A company is set up to develop Maglev (magnetic levitation trains).

Terex 33-11B earth-mover

1969 Last steam-hauled train runs in England.
1975 Italian Lella Lombardi becomes the first woman to drive in a season of Formula 1 Grand Prix races.
1976 British Railways introduces regular high-speed trains running at 125 mph.
1981 French TGV (Train à Grande Vitesse) enters service.
1983 Richard Noble in his jet car *Thrust II* reaches land speed record of 633 mph.
1984 Birmingham airport is linked with the railroad station by a 2,000 ft Maglev link, the world's first.
1985 Clive Sinclair introduces the unsuccessful battery-powered tricycle.called the Sinclair C5.
1987 Japanese Maglev train reaches 245 mph.

1988 GM "Sunrayer" solar-powered car attains 48 mph.
1990 21 million Beetles produced. No other car has been as popular.A French experimental TGV train reaches 320 mph.

Electric city bike

GLOSSARY

Airfoil On a high-performance vehicle, a wing, or part of one, which provides downthrust at speed, giving the vehicle better grip and allowing faster cornering.

Alloy wheel A lightweight wheel, usually made of metals like aluminum mixed with other materials (to form an alloy), to give strength.

Axle A rod or pin around which a wheel rotates; otherwise (in older vehicles or railroad wagons) it may be a rod or shaft connecting two wheels.

Bearing A mechanism allowing rotation between the hub of a wheel and its axle, or between an axle and its mounting on the vehicle. In modern vehicles, ball- or roller-bearings are most common.

Caboose An extra wagon on a construction train for carrying workers (or for horses when a horse-drawn streetcar returns downhill).

Camber The convex surface of a road, having the center raised above the curbs in order to drain the road more effectively.

Carbon fiber Very slender strands of pure carbon used to reinforce molded plastic articles, making them stronger and lighter than metal ones.

Carpentum A Roman two-wheeled carriage, used by wealthy women.

Chassis The frame of a vehicle, distinct from the bodywork, to which the engine, gearbox, and suspension are fitted.

Cisium A lightweight, two-wheeled Roman carriage, which could carry two people.

Conestoga A type of four-wheeled wagon used in the United States.

Cylinder The part of an engine where steam, or exploding vapor (in an internal combustion engine), forces out a piston which then drives the wheels.

Derailleur A gear-changing mechanism on a bicycle, in which the chain is moved from one size of toothed wheel (sprocket) to another.

Diesel engine A type of internal combustion engine. The fuel vapor is made to explode by a very high pressure reached in the cylinders.

Disk brake A brake which works by squeezing friction pads onto a smooth-faced disk coupled to the wheels.

Draft A word used to describe animals that pull loads.

Elliptical spring A curved, flexible strip of steel (or several bound together), fixed at each end, with an axle attached to the middle.

Felloe (also spelled felly) The curved rim, or part of the rim, of a wheel.

Flange (On railroad wheels) An extra part of the rim, at right angles to it, which helps keep the wagon on the rails.

Fossil fuels Fuels like coal, oil, or gas, which are formed from decayed plants or animals deep underground.

Fuel injection A way of feeding fuel into an internal combustion engine; gas or oil is squirted under high pressure, often directly into the cylinder.

Gearbox Allows the driver to adjust the speed and acceleration of the vehicle by changing how fast the wheels turn in relation to the engine. This can be done when the driver selects a gear or automatically.

Groma A Roman surveying instrument, consisting of plumb lines attached to the ends of a pair of crossed sticks; for setting up vertical lines and right angles.

Hub The center of a wheel, which rotates around the axle.

Internal combustion A type of engine where the fuel burns in the cylinder (unlike a steam engine, where it burns in the firebox).

Litter A sort of carriage, dating back to Roman times, which is carried by servants or slaves.

Livery For employees, a uniform, and for vehicles, any special color scheme indicating to whom the vehicle belongs.

Maglev - "magnetic levitation": a type of railway where the carriages hover over electric circuits which also propel them.

Monocoque A rigid hollow shell (like the body of a car) which is strong enough to hold the engine, gearbox, and suspension without a chassis.

Municipal Describes anything relating to the local government of a town or borough.

Pantograph A spring-loaded frame on top of an electric train or locomotive; it makes contact with the overhead wire and can be folded down when not in use.

Patent A legal document which gives inventors protection from other people using their ideas.

Pneumatic tire A hollow tire, blown up with compressed air. Virtually all tires used now are pneumatic.

Post Horn A long, straight brass or silver trumpet, sounded by 18th and 19th century coachmen to warn of their approach.

Supercharger An air pump, driven from an engine, which forces air and fuel into an engine, greatly increasing its power output.

Toll Fees collected from road travelers to pay for the upkeep of roads and bridges.

Treadle A flat pedal, which is pumped up and down to operate a machine. Old sewing machines had treadles.

Turbocharger Similar to a supercharger, but the pump is driven by a turbine placed in the engine's exhaust; turbochargers increase performance and economy.

Vacuum brake (as used on trains); each wheel has a brake, held by springs. To move off, air is drawn out of cylinders by a vacuum pipe running along the whole train. If the vacuum fails, the brakes work automatically.

Velocipede A term describing any early bicycle with pedals.

INDEX

PRINTED IN BELGIUM BY
proost
INTERNATIONAL BOOK PRODUCTION